# PAUL HINDEMITH

# A Concentrated Course in Traditional Harmony

## BOOK II

### Exercises for
### Advanced Students

*English Translation by*
ARTHUR MENDEL

New York
ASSOCIATED MUSIC PUBLISHERS, INC.
Schott & Co., Ltd., London          B. Schott's Söhne, Mainz

# PREFACE

The first book of this work, *Traditional Harmony,* in the ten years since it was first published, has proved a useful textbook. It has provided thousands of students with exercise material. The general approval accorded to the mode of presentation has been extended also to the nature and quality of the exercises. That book was intended as a very brief survey of traditional harmonic practice, without reference to any technique based on a more developed and more advanced theory of music. The provisional character of the book showed itself in another respect as well: although the harmonic material it offered is that which a composer who follows traditional paths uses every day, the first volume of *Traditional Harmony* made no particular point of developing specifically compositional exercises. In the first place the composer's gift of invention cannot be taught (although suitable exercises are indispensable to the uncovering and development of talent), and in the second place the book was of course intended for the general use of *all* harmony students and not for the special purposes of the budding composer.

But it developed that students adequately endowed with musical intelligence, but not with talent for composition, derived benefit from mastering the technical problems of *Traditional Harmony;* and then, since the nature of their gifts excluded genuinely creative activity, they regretfully had to give up this useful occupation with the technique of traditional harmony because any further source of appropriate nourishment for their alert intelligence was nowhere to be found. The indicated task then was to provide, for good, intelligent musicians who did not aspire to the laurels of the composer, exercise material that might spur them on to high technical achievements, but that at the same time would free them from the exacting feeling of creative obligation.

Such material is what the present book seeks to offer. It contains pieces of every type and scope. The exercises range, in medium of performance, from piano solo to string orchestra, and from solo voice to mixed chorus; structurally between little dance-pieces and full-grown

[iii]

sonata movements the technical essentials of many styles of writing will be found. The harmonic material is the same as that used in *Traditional Harmony, Book I*. The first five chapters of the new book correspond to Chapters IX-XIII of the old book, while the sixth chapter extends the material offered in its sixteenth (supplementary) chapter. For the treatment of this already familiar material, the present book offers the student many suggestions that lead him far beyond the primitive domain of mere technical proficiency, an objective to which *Book I* (and routine harmony instruction altogether) restricted itself. The present book, thus, performs approximately the function of a travel guide that one reads when a real journey cannot be undertaken.

Yet, the use of these exercises should not be confined to the intelligent non-composer. I have found that they are of the highest value for the indispensable technical training of the composer, although of course now and then a creative spirit will find itself uncomfortably cramped in the paths laid down for these composition-skeletons. But even a composer will find material enough (especially in the last exercises of the book) to arouse his imagination. Any intelligent musician can solve the problems here posed, but not everyone will be able to give them the spark of life that transforms them into real music.

Needless to say, these exercises, like the earlier ones, have grown out of class teaching, and have been thoroughly tried out in practice. Again it was a class in theory and composition at the School of Music of Yale University that helped me to find the solution of the problem.

Paul Hindemith

*New Haven, Connecticut*
*May 1953*

# CONTENTS

Preface . . . . . . . . . . . . . . iii

Chapter I    1

    Four Canons for String Quartet . . . . . . . 2
    Two Songs for Soprano (or Tenor) and Piano . . . . 4
    Two Three-Part Choruses . . . . . . . . . 5
    Two Songs for Four-Part Chorus . . . . . . . 7

Chapter II    10

    Two Songs for Mezzo-Soprano and Piano . . . . . 10
    Two Five-Part Choruses . . . . . . . . . 12

Chapter III    15

    Four Four-Part Choruses . . . . . . . . . 15
    Theme and Variations for String Trio . . . . . 18
    Three Pieces for Clarinet, English Horn, and Bassoon . . 20

Chapter IV    23

    Two Pieces for Viola and Piano . . . . . . . 23
    Three Scherzi for Trombone and Piano . . . . . 26

Chapter V    28

    Miniature Dances for Piano . . . . . . . . 29
    Three Pieces for Harmonium . . . . . . . . 31

Chapter VI    36

    Suite for String Orchestra . . . . . . . . 37
    Two Fugatos for Two Voices . . . . . . . 54
    Two Two-Part Instrumental Fugues . . . . . . 58
    Three Three-Part Vocal Fugues . . . . . . 60
    First Movement of a Sonata for Clarinet and Piano . . 64
    First Movement of a Sonata for Horn and Piano . . . 67
    Theme and Variations for String Quartet . . . . . 71

# CHAPTER I

Tonal and harmonic material for the pieces to be written in this chapter:

a. the tonic, dominant, and subdominant triads of the major and minor keys*;

b. the diatonic triads (major, minor, diminished, and augmented) on all the other degrees of the major and minor scales;

c. the dominant seventh chord with its three inversions;

d. the dominant harmonies derived from the dominant seventh chord: $V_9$, $V_7^{13}$, and their inversions;

e. the subdominant chord $II_5^6$.

In musical notation:

* *Note:* Terminology—capital letters = major (C = C-major triad);
small letters = minor (a = a-minor triad).

[1]

These are all chords that were worked with in Chapters I-IX of *Traditional Harmony, Book I.*

## Four Canons for String Quartet

These pieces are to be written on four staves, for two violins, viola, and 'cello—the viola in alto clef.

Two of the four voices are in canon: one of these is given, and the other is to be added. The entrance of the imitative second voice is indicated in each canon. In the first two pieces, it carries out its imitation at the octave below; in the third, at the fifth below; and in the fourth, at the major third above. In the first three canons the imitation reproduces every interval exactly; in the fourth a different treatment is prescribed.

The two voices forming the canon are to be worked out first, and the other two added only afterwards. The non-canonic voices must also take the form of logically developed and easily intelligible melodic lines: voices that act as mere filling are to be avoided. Nevertheless, the rhythmic activity of these voices must be kept from interfering with the two canonic voices' functioning as the subject of principal interest. Accordingly, in the first and fourth canons it will hardly be necessary to use note-values shorter than the ♩., while in the second and third the ♩ is to be regarded as the basic unit of motion.

In the third canon, the two canonic voices lie very close together in pitch. This means that the development of the tonality (f minor) depends mostly on the combined efforts of the given upper voice and the free bass.

In the fourth canon, particular attention must be paid to the melodic flow of the upper voice.

1. Fast (♩. = 120) Canon between First Violin and Viola

## 2. Moderate (♩ = 88) Canon between First Violin and 'Cello

## 3. Andante (♩ = 96) Canon between Second Violin and Viola

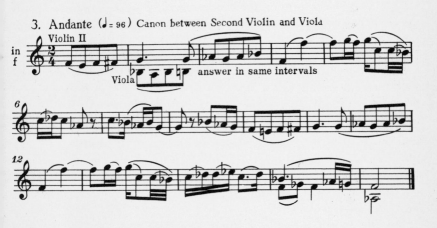

answer in same intervals

## 4. Allegretto (♩. = 76) Canon between 'Cello and Viola

answer with the tones of the D-major scale

# Two Songs for Soprano (or Tenor) and Piano
## on texts by William Blake (1757-1827)

### 1. Soft Snow
### 2. The Sick Rose

The mood suggested in the vocal line is to be intensified in the accompaniment, in accordance with the content of the poem. For this purpose, the suggested patterns of accompaniment should be carried on. This does not mean that the piano parts may contain nothing else. The effect of meaningless bustle which the uninterrupted repetition of a single accompaniment motif would create is to be avoided by one or more interpolations of other (quieter) motifs.

The dynamics are to be suited to the expression established by the solo voice and the accompaniment.

The accompaniment must suit the soprano version of each song as well as the tenor. Accordingly, it must avoid tones or figures in either the soprano or the tenor register that would disturb the vocal line. (Be careful with non-chord tones.) Furthermore, the line consisting of the uppermost tones of the accompaniment must, although interrupted by other tones, have a certain melodic quality which in the case of a tenor singing the vocal part would permit this succession of prominent points to be understood as the upper outline of the total structure.

## 1. Soft Snow

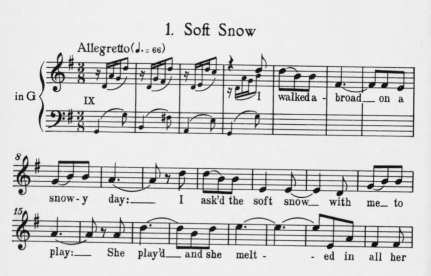

in G

snow-y day:____ I ask'd the soft snow__ with me__ to

play:____ She play'd__ and she melt - - ed in all her

prime, And the win - - ter___ call'd___ it___

___ a dread-ful crime._____

## 2. The sick Rose

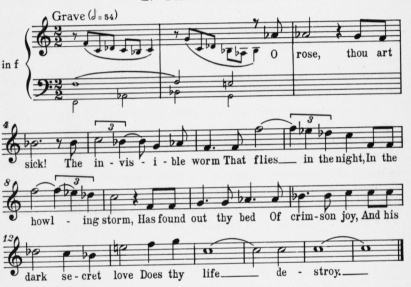

Grave (♩ = 54)

in f

O rose, thou art

sick! The in - vis - i - ble worm That flies___ in the night, In the

howl - ing storm, Has found out thy bed Of crim-son joy, And his

dark se - cret love Does thy life___ de - stroy.___

**Two Three-Part Choruses for Soprano, Alto, and Tenor**

1. Song      Robert Browning (1812-1889)
2. The Vine      James Thomson (1834-1882)

The lowest part, as the foundation of the harmony and the tonal development, is to be written first. Since it lies in the tenor voice, and thus moves in a comparatively high register (for the most part in the small octave), strong bass effects are to be avoided. These are not really effective except in the true bass register, sung by bass voices. In the tenor they mostly give the impression of unnatural imitations of a bass. Therefore, instead of the strong leaps of fourths and fifths charac-

[5]

teristic of the bass, it will be better to use the more melodic progressions of seconds and thirds.

In the first song, harmonize measures 6-8 differently from the corresponding measures 1-3. The unit of motion is the ♩. . Too many eighth-notes in the middle or lowest voice would rob the top voice of its melodic importance, and easily result in a contrapuntal texture that would not suit the lightness of the poem and of the melodic line.

To achieve an appropriate and convincing realization of the second song, the very fast tempo must not be weighed down by note-values smaller than half-notes (♩) or triplet half-notes (♩♩♩). One must also clearly understand the metric structure of the piece in order to place the principal harmonies of the tonality at the best points. The piece falls into groups of two or three measures, in each of which one measure is felt as accented and therefore demanding harmonic and tonal preference. To understand this, divide the piece up into the aforementioned two- and three-measure groups. However, to realize the full effect of the *crescendo* in measures 13-20, it will be necessary to give up any accentuation in the course of those measures; try to get along without any of the principal harmonies of the tonality, and avoid as much as possible the recurrence of harmonies just heard.

This exercise cannot be looked upon as solved until the class has demonstrated its usefulness and practicability by singing it. *Afterwards,* the pieces may be played at the piano for practice in score-reading.

## 1. Song

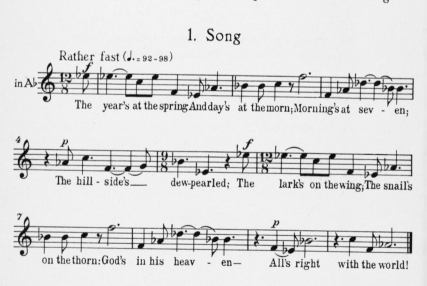

## 2. The Vine

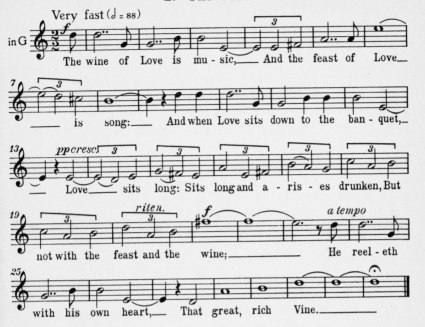

Very fast (♩ = 88)

in G

The wine of Love is mu-sic,___ And the feast of Love___ ___ is song:___ And when Love sits down to the ban-quet,___ Love___ sits long: Sits long and a-ris-es drunken, But not with the feast and the wine;___ He reel-eth with his own heart,___ That great, rich Vine.___

## Two Songs for Four-Part Chorus of Mixed Voices
### on texts by William Shakespeare (1564-1616)

1. **Winter**
2. **Orpheus**

Although the only task in these two songs is to complete the harmonies, it is possible by adroit leading and rhythmic treatment of the lower voices to intensify the expression proper to each song in a considerable degree.

Write on four separate staves, the three upper voices in the c-clefs:

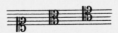

Sing the songs in chorus; then play the score on the piano.

[7]

# 1. Winter

## 2. Orpheus

For the second verse, the rhythm of the melody is to be changed as necessary:

> Every thing that heard him play,
> Even the billows of the sea,
>> Hung their heads and then lay by.
> In sweet music is such art,
> Killing care and grief of heart
>> Fall asleep, or, hearing, die.

# CHAPTER II

The chord material for this chapter corresponds to that in Chapter X of *Book I*. In addition to the harmonies previously used, we now adopt the secondary seventh chords on I, II, III, IV, VI, and VII of the major and minor scales, with their inversions.

In musical notation:

## Two Songs for Mezzo-Soprano and Piano

1. **Memory**      **William Browne (1588-1643)**
2. **Epitaph**      **Robert Herrick (1591-1674)**

Write the solo voice in 𝄞 or (for practice) in one of the c-clefs that embrace the range of that voice: ( 𝄡 or 𝄡 ). For the first song, an accompaniment figure in eighth-notes is recommended, in which melodic development must be suppressed in favor of broken chords. The dynamic rise and fall of the vocal line must be supported by careful gradations in the fullness of the chords, i. e., in the number of tones contained in each harmony, which may be increased by doublings.

In the song, "Epitaph", variety may be introduced into the accompaniment by the use of different registers of the piano: low chords may be juxtaposed against high ones. For this purpose it is not necessary to cling literally either to the particular octave in which the bass voice is written or to its rhythm.

In both songs the seventh chords will have to be treated with considerable caution. When the voice has the seventh of a chord, one will have to ask oneself whether the accompaniment should include the seventh in the same octave, or, in fact, whether it need include it at all. If the figures call for a seventh that can only occur in the accompaniment, one must consider carefully in which octave it will be most effective.

Try to work out a typically pianistic style; avoid the normal four-part texture of schoolbook harmony exercises.

Add precise dynamic markings.

## 1. Memory

## 2. Epitaph
### Upon a Child that died

## Two Five-Part Choruses for Mixed Voices

1. **Man**             John Davies (1569-1626)
2. **The Return of Spring**    Anonymous (ca. 1200-1300)

In the first song the only technical difficulty will be the task of compressing the five voices within a comparatively narrow compass.

The second one poses different problems. Here a well-flowing upper voice must be invented for the first 16 measures. This voice is to be written first, and is to be felt as the principal melody, forcing the bass into the somewhat less important role of the lower framing voice. Measures 17-22 are to be treated as a refrain, contrasted in texture, expression, and dynamics with the first part. Beginning with measure 23, four measures of this refrain are repeated, this time with the tenor as principal voice.

The fifth voice which is to be added to the usual four-part choral texture (soprano, alto, tenor, bass), may be either a second soprano or a second tenor (baritone). Write on five staves, using as many different clefs as possible.

Don't forget to sing both songs. Then play them on the piano.

*Note on the second song:* "Is it really necessary to set Latin texts to music? When shall we ever have occasion to use this dead language?"

Answer: Old-fashioned musicians may be able to get along, in smug self-satisfaction, with whatever happens to lie nearest at hand. But ought we not to strive to learn something beyond the bare technical necessities of everyday life? To anyone who has no notion of the Latin language and of the way it has been treated in music, almost all music before 1500, as well as an important branch of later music, must remain a closed book. But it is just the music of the period before 1500, as has been shown so often in the last decades, that represents for the musician of today an inexhaustible source of stimulation and enlightenment, at least as important as the music of the eighteenth and nineteenth centuries, and in many respects more so.

For this song as well as for those to follow (in Chapter VI) the student should become familiar with the rules of syllable-division in Latin.

## 1. Man

# 2. The Return of Spring

Translation (for information only; not for practical use):

Winter time, farewell!
Summer nears with joy,
With warmth and with beauty,
Which are summer's sure signs.
The earth flowers as always,
The lilies blossom forth,
The roses exude fragrance,
The poultry cackles.

# CHAPTER III

Simple alteration. To the harmonic material hitherto used, we now add:

a. triads derived from the changeable sixth and seventh degrees of the melodic minor scale:

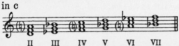

II III IV V VI VII

b. the similarly derived secondary seventh chords:

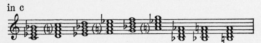

c. in major, the chords:

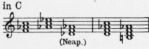

d. in minor, the chords:

These and similar tonal constructions are discussed in Chapter XI of *Book I.*


### Four Poems from the Rubáiyát of Omar Khayyám
*(translated by Edward FitzGerald, 1809-1883)*
### for Four-Part Chorus of Mixed Voices

In each of the four pieces, the melody, of which only fragments are given, must first be completed. Avoid using the piano or any other instrument. Nor may the melodies be completed by merely adding tones which more or less fit. On the contrary, the student must force himself to fill the gaps by *singing*, and must not write anything down until he has arrived at the final form of the melodies vocally. Here, as

[15]

elsewhere in this book, "singing" does not mean just humming under one's breath, but really singing out, with the words—the one and only way to cultivate the feeling for the organic growth of melodic lines. Once one has become used to such singing, one cannot fail to recognize the hair-raising absurdity of lessons in musical "theory" that limit themselves to the keyboard and staff-paper, and in so doing choke and dry up the natural source of all musical utterances, the most reliable and inspiring regulating factor of musical intentions—the human voice.

When the melodic line has been completed, the bass is to be added first, and then the other voices. Try to raise these songs from the realm of mere harmony exercises into the domain of intense musical expression, by reinforcing the poetic quality of the words through

the varying speed of the chordal succession;

the stressing or suppressing of melodies and harmonies; and

the choice of quieter or more agitated, stepwise or skipping motion.

The beginning of the first quatrain, with its joyous "Come, fill the Cup", calls for strength and buoyancy of tonality and motion, while the gradual fading of the optimism in the text must be matched by a similar abatement of all the musical elements.

The second quatrain can remain throughout on the expressive level of resignation—an effect to be achieved mainly by stepwise motion and the frequent repetition of quiet but expressive motifs.

"There was the Door" had best be set to loud, heavy chords, which may mainly follow the rhythmic arrangement: 𝅝 𝅗𝅥 . At the words "and then", in measure 9, the Neapolitan sixth chord may be used to occupy the whole measure and a little more, leading, with the melody, to a *piano* ending.

In the fourth quatrain, the heavy-spirited hesitation suggested in the sketch is to be brought out both in melody and harmony.

In these pieces, as well as in the later ones of this chapter and in those of Chapters IV and V, great care must be taken *not* to modulate. Only by avoiding modulation can the tonal style aimed at in these exercises be achieved. The prescribed harmonic material is not to be added to, and no cadential formations are to be used except the half and full cadences proper to the tonality of each piece. Since the technique of employing altered chords is all too apt to slide off into tonal uncertainty and disorder, precautions against such dangers must be taken by the use of recurrent tonic harmonies, and by the wise placing of these and the other principal harmonies of the key, so that the hearer may not lose the tonal thread.

[16]

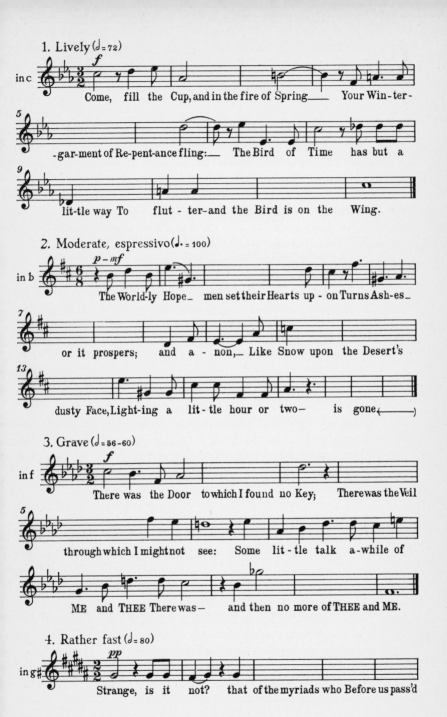

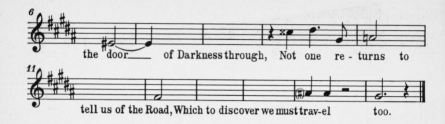

the door___ of Darkness through, Not one re - turns to

tell us of the Road, Which to discover we must trav-el too.

## Theme and Variations for String Trio
### *(Violin, Viola, and 'Cello)*

The theme, as well as each of the three variations, consists of three different thematic groups which must be clearly differentiated in texture and harmony. Thus, measures 7-8 and 13-14 will be similar to measures 1-2, and there will be correspondences between 3-4 and 9-10, and between 5-6 and 11-12.

In the first variation, measures 15-18 and the corresponding later groups are to be treated as an accompanied solo for viola. In the intervening measures, the alternation of the motifs suggested in the sketch must come out clearly. But be careful not to let any too striking similarity in these passages to measures 33-34 and 39-40 of the second variation, or to the principal motif of the third (measures 43-44, etc.), make itself disturbingly noticeable.

### Three Pieces for Clarinet (in A), English Horn, and Bassoon

In the first piece begin by writing the top (clarinet) part. The lowest voice here given moves in definitely melodic fashion, even though it does little more than set forth the most important tonal functions—tonic, both dominants, leading tone, Neapolitan—by means of broken chords and intervals. It would be a mistake to set a really independent top voice against this pseudo-melodic life (which strongly attracts our attention through linear accumulation of many tones), for this would force our perceptive faculties to take in two factors of equal weight. Doubtless the best solution will be to invent a line moving in half-notes and quarter-notes for measures 1-9 and 17-25—a line possessing enough life of its own to be felt as an independent melody, and yet one that will leave the bass sufficient freedom for its rhythmic and melodic activity. Under such circumstances, the middle voice will of course have to remain quite subdued.

Measures 10-16 are to be treated as a contrasting middle section, and since in the opening and closing sections we have decided on a juxtaposition of lines which, despite the limitations described, have a certain independence, it will be sensible to adopt for the middle section a homophonic texture in which either all three voices have essentially the same rhythm or else two similar voices are set off against a contrasting quieter one moving in half-notes.

The two other pieces are to be treated in similar fashion. In the second one, the lowest voice has a definite solo character. In the third it will be best to bring out very clearly the structural articulation: measures 1-4, principal material; 5-10, subsidiary and transitional; 10-13, principal material; 14-17, coda; 18-20, confirmation of the ending.

3. Rather slow ($\quad$ = 88-92)

in a

# CHAPTER IV

We shall now practice the incorporation of secondary dominants into the tonal material we have used hitherto. The definition given in *Book I* may here be repeated:

"Any major or minor triad other than the tonic triad of a key (II, III, IV, V, VI in major; IV, V, VI in minor), as well as all major or minor triads created by alteration, can be emphasized by being preceded by a triad (major, less frequently minor) or seventh chord (mostly of the dominant seventh type—that is, consisting of major triad and minor seventh) which stands in the relation of a dominant to it.

"These secondary dominant chords contain tones which do not belong to the main key (or, what amounts to the same thing, alterations of the tones of the key).

"The dominant seventh chord of the main key can also be preceded by its dominant. . . .

"The effect of a secondary dominant can be created not only by a chord standing in the relation of dominant to its successor, but also by a chord erected on a tone which is used as the leading tone to the root of the following chord, thus establishing an artificial VII, $VII_6$, $VII_4^6$, or $VII_7$ (altered or unaltered, in root position or any inversion)."

### Two Pieces for Viola and Piano

1. **Andante**
2. **Very lively**

First mark all the places where secondary dominants can be introduced. Then determine under which tones of the given melody the principal harmonies of the key are to stand. When these two series of imaginary harmonies are compared, it will be easy to determine how many members of the first series can be used to support the second. Since tonal clarity is always the first requirement, we must be careful not to take too many members of the first series into our tonal plan:

they would become preponderant, and diminish the value of even the principal harmonies of the key. Secondary dominants, even when used sparingly, always result in sudden tonal fits and starts. They are typical representatives of tonal megalomania: they try to represent something that they are not, employing the means of modulation but not having the force to produce the conviction of modulation. The effect of rapid twists and turns without basic change of tonal direction reminds one of a bicycle wobbling zigzag down the street, instead of either going straight or describing well-arched curves. The use of secondary dominants in quantity evokes the tonal structure of the second- and third-class music of the past century, or—when they are added to appropriate melodies—of the syrupy sentimentality of many of the popular and "semi-popular" pieces of the present day, which, tonally speaking, are frequently nothing but chains of secondary dominants. These styles of music show clearly how a technical device that is perfectly good but by no means everywhere usable becomes threadbare when it is over-used, and ends up by being ridiculous and repulsive. For practice, we can of course experiment in the following pieces to see how far the increasing number of secondary dominants strengthens construction and contributes to clear understanding, and just when they begin to degenerate into a mere spineless series of insipid curlicues.

In the first piece, make a clear distinction between the structural sections by using different textures in the piano part. After the first appearance of the principal material, measures 11-19 require different treatment. From measure 20 on, return to a modified form of the texture used for the principal material. The final measures, beginning with measure 32, are to be treated as a coda. Precise dynamic indications are to be included.

In the second piece, too, the two parts are to be clearly differentiated in texture. The given voice is to be left entirely to the viola, which even in the *da capo* is to play just what is given. The piano, on the other hand, is to play in the *da capo* the melody of the second part, provided with an accompaniment, and transposed to the tonic key A.

1. Andante (♩ = 66)

## Three Scherzi for Trombone and Piano

What was said about the working out of the preceding pieces applies to these as well.

In measures 4 and 18 of the first piece, the B-major harmony is to be treated as a Neapolitan chord (i. e., really C♭).

In the second piece, the progressions from secondary dominant to secondary tonic are to be assigned mainly to the two-eighth figure ( ♪♫ ) in the accompaniment.

The suggested model for the accompaniment of the third piece is *not* applicable to measures 9-14.

Needless to say, playing the finished pieces may here again be regarded as the basis for final judgment of them. If no trombone is available, use some other instrument as a substitute.

2. Allegro assai (♩. = 96)

in B♭

1.  2.

p cresc.

3. Pesante (♩ = 100)

in C

① ② ③ ④

① 

① ② ③ ④ ① with Piano in octaves

Pattern for the accompaniment:

[27]

# CHAPTER V

The chords to be added to our material in this lesson—those that are inserted in a tonality by means of the so-called *extended* or *chromatic alteration*—are explained in most harmony textbooks as follows:

> Every tone of a scale can be chromatically altered, and the altered tones can form parts of chords that may be regarded as belonging to the key.

These chords must follow the basic law of traditional harmony, according to which every harmony can be reduced to an original close position in which it is built up out of thirds of some sort, and essentially belongs to one of the basic types of chords with which we began our harmony exercises: triads of four kinds, dominant seventh chords, secondary seventh chords, and ninth chords. When we subject these "altered" chords to the operations we used on the original triads, etc.—namely inversion, replacement of one of the chord factors by its neighboring tone, use as secondary dominant—we come into possession of the entire arsenal of this late style of traditional harmonic and tonal development.

This is not the place to expose the weaknesses of the technique of alteration and of its theoretical foundation. Suffice it to say that all chords of this sort are simply derivatives and variants of the dominant seventh chord. This concise and complete definition—which, incidentally, was formulated as early as the eighteenth century, but, like so many of the clearest and simplest explanations of tonal phenomena, was disregarded and forgotten in favor of hazier interpretations—was drawn upon in *Traditional Harmony, Book I,* where the derivations and uses of these chords are described in Chapter XIII.

Nevertheless a list of the chords there given may be repeated here:

in C, on each chromatic degree

etc.

Still other chords may be formed in the indicated fashion, but they are nothing but notational variants of chords already familiar. There are in addition, it is true, a great number of chords that are not covered by the method described. Our traditional theory of harmony cannot give satisfactory rules either for their construction or for their use. Anyone who wishes to use them must either trust to his musical instinct—a procedure that does not necessarily lead to convincing results—or look around for a system which, reaching out further than the methods hitherto in use, will comprehend, explain, and arrange in order *all* conceivable harmonies. But in the present course of study of *traditional* harmony there is, in any case, no place for such chords.

## Miniature Dances for Piano

Modulation—i. e., the establishment of new tonics, which would be felt as independent—is still not to be used.

First write a bass line that moves along well, and then fill in the other tones of the harmony.

3. Jig in C♯ (♩. = 92)

4. Polka in F (♩ = 120)

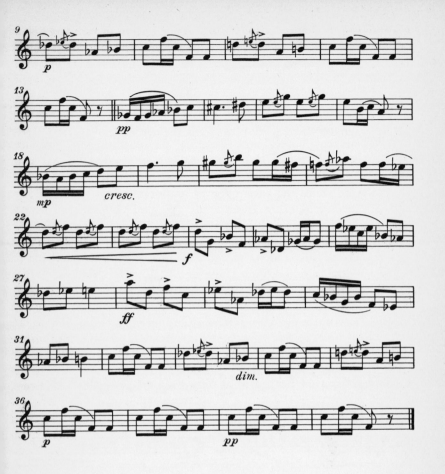

## Three Pieces for Harmonium

1. Melancholy
2. Scherzando
3. Resignation

Harmonium?!?! But aren't we musicians of some culture, and haven't we better, more reliable instruments at our disposal, better adapted to serious musical exercises than that primitive old wheeze-box?

I will be frank to state that I consider the harmonium an educational medium of very high rank, and that for purposes of instruction it seems to me almost indispensable. What I have in mind is not a harmonium with six or more sounding stops and numerous other devices, but rather the harmonium in its least pretentious form, without stops, and with no added features except a single crescendo-swell device—the form in which, as the simplest descendant of the old regal, it ekes out its existence, scorned by musicians, in the homes of sentimental music-lovers and the humble chapels of the smallest congregations. Of course it lacks almost everything that would assure it a place in the ranks of "respectable" musical instruments, but it has two characteristics that will teach the student of the technique of musical writing more about the connection of tones and harmonies than any piano or group of other instruments: its tones continue to sound with constant volume, and they are not susceptible to accentuation.

But is not treasuring such a pitiful instrument like preaching the virtue of poverty and the moral value of asceticism to one living in luxury? The counter-question might be: Why not, if that will further the development of the individual and the general welfare?

The tones of the harmonium, continuing to sound with constant volume, present every chord throughout its entire duration in an unchanging distribution of volume and sound quality. Other instruments (except the organ) do not do this. Either they subordinate the strength and expression of the individual chord tones in varying degree to the requirements of voiceleading and other performance factors, or, as with the piano, their tones rapidly die away after a sharp initial attack. In both cases a chord is subjected to continual structural changes in the course of its duration. Roughnesses in the harmonic path are smoothed over by changes of tone-color, dynamics, vibrato, etc.; insipid and inexpressive harmonies are livened up by similiar means and endowed with greater intensity. Thus what we are used to looking upon as simple harmonic or tonal effects are in reality the products of a complicated and by no means constant combination of many factors. But for a true knowledge of harmonies and their possibilities it is of the highest importance to have them available for experimental purposes in a form free from all adulteration. For this the harmonium is the ideal instrument. A chord that starts out as a hideous harmony sounds forth in unmitigated hideousness until the entrance of the next one—and equally, a euphonious combination remains continuously perceptible in its euphony. The harmonies are heard in undeceptive nudity, and nothing can be added to them or subtracted from them.

Even more important is the impossibility of accented playing on the harmonium. As performing musicians, we are terribly spoiled.

What we hear, play, and sing is in almost every instance clearly articulated according to its metric structure. Musical form, with its divisions down to the last detail of alternation between strong and weak beats, is caught in a net of lines like the degrees of latitude and longitude on a global map, which tell us at any moment exactly what part of the form we have reached. Valuable as this constant information is for the understanding of music by the hearer or the performer, it has made us in the course of time so dependent on metric division that it has become almost impossible for us to grasp melodies without imposing metric pattern on them, let alone understand larger forms without clear accentuation—just as we can hardly listen to melodic lines without unconsciously supplying harmonies to go with them. The harmonium, if we understand it fully and make sensible use of it, can in its expressionless neutrality make meter and rhythm our servants again (as they should naturally be, and as they were in former times), instead of letting us run nervously to and fro as their slaves, in the chains of eternal regularity of accent. To a certain degree, one sort of accent can be imitated on the harmonium—namely, that which is produced by the mere increase of loudness (dynamic accent). I am not referring to the opening of a little shutter by means of the knee lever: that unimportant device has only insignificant influence on the playing of the instrument. Dynamic increase has to be accomplished by increasing the number of tones, not the volume of the single tone. A structural accent of rhythm or meter must thus be expressed through a chord that contains a greater number of tones than its unaccented neighbors. Thus the composer—and not, as in all other cases, the performer—is directly responsible for making the form fully clear.

I have no wish in this connection to play the part of a fool who in joy over his hobby-horse becomes its prophet, and who wholly overlooks what must, despite all the advantages of the instrument, be recognized as its primitiveness and its undeniable practical limitations (which come close to making it unusable). But I would recommend even to the doubter that he once give himself without prejudice to the pursuit of the lines of thought suggested here, and then work out these pieces and play them through with an extremely critical ear. Anyone who does so seriously and with a mind open to an appreciation of the problems outlined will be surprised at the difficulty of the assignment; and I am sure that he will not let the matter rest with this one attempt. Exercises written for the harmonium, like choral settings, should be standard devices in the teaching of the technique of musical writing. (Of course, the organ serves the same purpose, but what harmony or counterpoint class has an organ at its constant disposal?)

Let us stretch the limited expressive material offered by the harmonium to its utmost, and squeeze out of it every expressive possibility it embodies. Our first piece is to place the hearer in a mood of deepest melancholy; the second shall make him gay; and the third shall suggest sorrowful resignation. It is difficult to describe just how a listener who is willing to yield to such moods can be persuaded—what the specific technical means must be, among the chord material available to us, that will lead with some certainty to the experiencing of the moods named. Although this could be established by lengthy psychological experiments in people's reactions to different forms of writing, it must be left to the student to find out by actual trial what and how he must write. It seems perhaps unfair to leave him so suddenly to his own devices; but the moment he leaves purely technical things behind, and turns his attention more to the emotional effects of music, he will be obliged, like all musicians before him, to rely more and more on his own powers of imagination, or to find his stimuli in available models. Whichever method he chooses, he must always in such work have uppermost in mind the emotional effect to be produced, and suit the technical treatment of the material entirely to that effect. Of course, the combination of so absurd an apparatus as a harmonium with the sublime mood of resignation is too grotesque to be taken really seriously. But if the purpose (or at least the inevitable effect) of music is to awaken some sort of feelings in the listener, there seems no reason why it should not be realized with any sound-producing medium that can be bent at all in this direction (which with a xylophone, for example, would not be quite so simple). If this goal can be reached with our harmonium, it is to be assumed that we shall be all the more able to do so with more flexible and expressive means.

In respect to harmony and tonality, our pieces will inevitably sound like so many hundreds of the sentimental *genre* pieces of the post-*Tristan* style. This is the fault not of any mania for imitation on our part, or on the part of all the composers who have written such pieces before us, but simply of the fact that the continuous use of "altered" dominant harmonies must always produce this type of expression. What was originally felt to be so "modern" and to promise so much, turns out to be a technical device that is useful only for the creation of all too limited effects. Nevertheless, it is advisable once, for practice, to wallow thoroughly in this style of writing if only to learn through exaggeration what in the end one wants to avoid, and thus to escape the danger of becoming an unconscious victim of harmonic progressions, the effect of which, for lack of experience gained through such practice, one had not clearly enough foreseen.

3. Resignation (♩ = 40)

# CHAPTER VI

From now on, all the material of traditional harmonic practice, including modulation, is at our disposal. Concerning the technique of modulating, see Chapters XIV and XV of *Traditional Harmony, Book I*.

### Suite for String Orchestra

**Fast**
**Arioso**
**Minuet**
**Finale—Very fast**

This suite is to be written for the usual string orchestra combination (Violins I and II, Violas, 'Celli, and Basses) on five staves.

Before starting work, read carefully the following instructions, and become thoroughly familiar with the kind of thinking that underlies them. This is indispensable for the proper solution of the problems given.

In what follows, I describe the working procedure as applied to a single movement (the first one in this suite) as a model, and this precisely and in great detail, since the same procedure is to be followed for each of the subsequent examples.

To many readers it may seem that the labor involved is out of all proportion to what is certainly not an excessively rich musical harvest—the more so since this book claims to deal with problems of traditional harmonic practice, and certainly none of the old textbooks contain anything of the exaggerated analyses and manipulations here offered. Others may consider the intrusion of the hyper-technical into the intimate sphere of their own harmonic and tonal imagination to be altogether disturbing or even insulting. Of course I am conscious of such objections, but I reject them flatly. I have enough familiarity with the inspirational side of compositional work, as well as its technical aspects, to know that such resistances are only the escapes and excuses of those who have never thought their musical ideas through to the end, and who have never achieved a fully effective working technique. Anyone who is disturbed by technical considerations in his work has simply not acquired sufficient technique. Good creative ideas can never be spoiled by the kind of comprehensive technique that has become unconscious through constant practice. On the contrary, only such a technique can bring them to the full realization of their possibilities. What I describe here is nothing but the making conscious of many procedures in the technique of musical writing which are generally followed anyway, but the underlying reasons for which are usually not subjected to the verdict of conscious deliberation. To do so is in no way to profane private sanctuaries, but simply to decrease the possible sources of error.

*Form.* The movement we are here considering consists of five structural elements, each distinct in character, expression, structural function, and technical treatment.

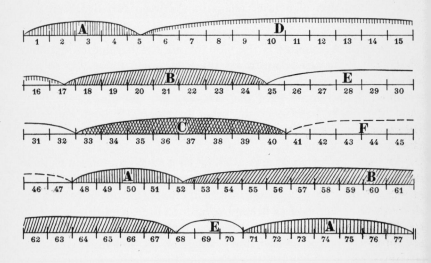

The first theme, A, appears three times (measures 1-5, 48-52, 71-77). It is, by virtue of its melodic structure, its position, and its external energy, structurally the most important material of the movement. Every time it appears it retains, despite varying dynamics, all its characteristic traits.

Of almost equal importance but different expression is B (second theme). It makes its first appearance as a triple iteration of a single melodic phrase (measures 17-25). At its second appearance (measures 52-68) it is hardly changed in expression, but it has been extended to the length of 16 half-notes, and it now consists of two longer iterations (instead of the three original short ones).

Material C, closely related to the main theme, A, forms the climax of the movement. It consists of a single phrase stated three times, each time with different tonal significance.

The other three elements are of lesser importance.

Element D fills the space between the first and second themes. It employs motifs derived from the first theme, and thus serves to make the listener better acquainted with the principal material while at the same time he is being led away from it.

Element E, which appears twice (measures 25-32 and 68-70) is simply a connecting member, and thus has no strong melodic individuality. What linear vitality it has it achieves by the continuous repetition of a single two-tone motif.

Even less independent is the transitional section, F, which has only the function of a brief relaxation between two significant elements.

*Tonality.* A tonality is the sum of all the harmonies that our analytic hearing can relate to a central harmony (tonic). To be perceived as a tonal grouping understandable in itself, a series of harmonies must be so arranged that the harmony intended as the tonic gains the upper hand over the other harmonies through cadences, favorable position, recurrent appearance, and support by its most closely related harmonies.

The tonality of a piece as a whole consists of a number of such individual tonal groupings, connected by more or less extended modulations. Modulation is accomplished by the use of groups of harmonies that can be understood as belonging both to the key of origin and to the key of destination. These common middle sections can in some circumstances be compressed into a single chord, and in special cases an apparently complete lack of connection between two tonalities may be advisable.

The present piece consists partly of sections in which a single tonality must appear with great definiteness, and partly of others which contrast with these stable tonal arrangements by their tonal vagueness. Even in these tonally weaker sections tonics can still be discovered, but they come in such quick succession that it is hard to find a common tonal denominator for them all. (If one were to attempt to fill a piece with nothing but this sort of tonal material, one would be approximately in the position of an architect trying to construct walls and supports out of a pudding-like mass.)

The following sketch illustrates the tonal design of this movement.

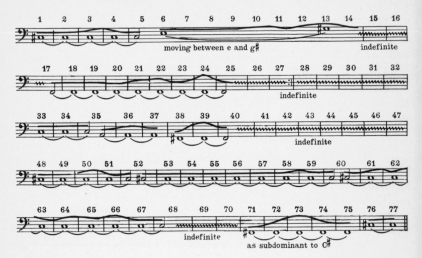

C♯* takes first place because of its numerical preponderance and preferred position at the beginning and end, apart from any other considerations. Since it is thus felt to be the tonic, there would be little point in seeking to oppose its superiority. Try rather to use its most closely related harmonies to create further solid support for it; and in addition, introduce occasional C♯ harmonies into the sections we have termed "indefinite."

The next most important tonality is F (measures 17-25). It would be well to reinforce that key, too.

Shorter sections of settled tonality occur in the middle of the piece, based on C, A, and F♯ (measures 33-40). Another group, near the end of the piece (71-77), based on F♯, ought not to become too independent. Try to make it as clear as possible that this F♯ is the subdominant of the final C♯; this can be accomplished by the use of C♯ and G♯ harmonies (despite the G♮ in the melody) or even of the tones C♯ and G♯ in other chords.

Measures 6-14 should leave unsettled the question which tonic, E or G♯, is felt to predominate, and in the rest of the piece, as has

* In the following statements no distinction is made between major and minor forms of tone names designating tonalities. The tonic harmonies of a tonality may appear in either form, depending on the student's discretion and on structural exigencies.

already been mentioned, no clear tonality is necessary.

*Tonal Amplitude.* By this term we mean the degree of tonal tension that exists within a clearly established tonal structure between the tonic chord and every other chord that bears a relation to it. The harmonies most closely related to the tonic (I V I, I VI IV I, . . .) produce only mild tonal deflections. The widest deflections we can achieve with the material at our disposal are represented by the use of secondary dominants preceding altered chords.

A glance at the first five measures of the movement under discussion will show what is meant. The two given voices call for chords that in the first two measures remain in the regions of close tonal connection with C♯ (I, VI, IV . . .); but from the third measure on they branch out more widely, with altered chords and their dominants. The heavy lines drawn into our sketch of tonal design show approximately how the tonal amplitude should be disposed: a horizontal course indicates little or no deflection, and the degree of deviation from the horizontal shows the degree of deflection from the momentary tonic. Places like the long C♯ of measures 48-68, or the long F♯ (17-25), which appear in the tonal whole as points of tonal rest complete in themselves, are endowed by the varying degrees of deflection with a rich *intra-tonal* life. Here, as in the use of all the other technical factors to be discussed, the rule is: if one element in the writing is to be most prominent, reduce the value of the others.

In the passages marked "indefinite", no tonal amplitude is indicated. Since in these passages one cannot tell precisely which tonic is in effect at any given moment, it is even less possible to determine such deflections.

*Harmonic Fluctuation.* This term indicates the differences in tension between one individual harmony and another. The harmony of least tension is the major triad; the harmonies of greatest tension within our traditional material are the chromatic alterations of the dominant seventh chord (see page 28). Harmonic fluctuation is *not* identical with tonal amplitude, although of course in the complete tonal effect neither is conceivable without the other. Chords of slight tonal deflection may be of a high degree of fluctuation, as for example a chord based on the tonic but forming a complicated harmony:

in C

On the other hand, a very wide tonal amplitude can be effected with a very simple harmony:

in C

In determining the fluctuation value of chords, one simply disregards the non-chord tones. Acquire the habit of carefully calculating harmonic fluctuation. Chords of high tension should not occur merely as the result of following the path of least resistance in the voice-leading; and a sudden relaxation of tension after progressions of chords of high tension is advisable only when one considers the resulting harmonic shock aesthetically justified.

Tonics of tonalities are best embodied in chords of no tension, which are also best suited to make the function of the subdominant most clear. Dominants, on the other hand (not to mention leading tones), can bear chords of high tension.

Here is a plan of fluctuation that will be easy to realize on the basis of the tonal outline previously given:

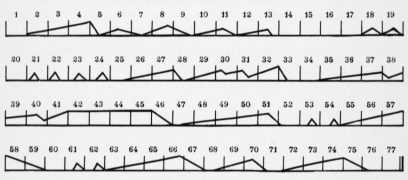

The heavy horizontal line represents harmonies without tension. From that level one rises to various degrees of harmonic fluctuation, the degree of tension being suggested by the degree of elevation of the jagged line, so far as such subtle procedures can be symbolized at all in visual or verbal representation.

*Harmonic Density.* This is another important factor to be calculated in the harmonic and tonal layout of the form. It has to do with the durations of the individual harmonies. The pattern of these durations does not, of course, necessarily coincide with the rhythm we perceive as that of the actual note durations brought about by the movement of the voices. If, for example, we were to harmonize the first two measures of this movement as follows:

the actual rhythmic movement would consist of the values:

while the harmonic motion would exhibit only:

The speed of movement of these harmonic note-values is what counts in the calculation of harmonic density. In this calculation, as in that of fluctuation, non-chord tones are simply disregarded.

To our plan of harmonic fluctuation given above, a plan of harmonic density may now be added:

Measures:
1- 5

6 -16

17-24

25-32

33-40

41-47

48-51

52-59

60-67

68-70

71-77

[43]

It will be seen that the main themes are set to the longer harmonies, which give them weight and significance, while the split-up rhythms (shorter harmonies) are used for the transitional, less independent sections.

In measures 25-32, and 68-70, one of the middle voices should be given the syncopated rhythm: ♪ ♪ ♪ ♪ ♪ ♪ , etc. In this way the actual rhythm of the voices will appear superimposed upon the half-note movement of the harmonic density:

*Style.* Within the framework of all the suggestions already made, we are still free to choose whether in the harmonic and tonal arrangement of our piece the combinations of tones are to be emphasized in a more harmonic or more melodic direction—whether, in other words, we wish to make the piece lean more toward homophonic or toward contrapuntal style. Neither of the extremes—simple, block-like harmonization, on the one hand, nor the greatest possible melodic independence of the added voices, on the other—seems possible for this movement. For a straight chordal harmonization, the whole structure, as determined by the main lines already established, is too complicated at the outset: it would only do violence to the fairly detailed melodic and harmonic design given in the sketch and would force an artificial simplification on it. But a definitely contrapuntal style would add further complications to the plan already sketched, and thus (in the quick tempo of the piece, which is not favorable to the understanding of too independent voice-leading) lay heavy burdens on the perceptive faculties of the hearer. Accordingly, it will be best to choose a style lying midway between the two extremes, and to let the writing veer now to the contrapuntal and now to the homophonic side, according to the character and significance of the individual sections of the structure.

Section A, each time it appears, may have fairly independent lines (as suggested in the version of the two opening measures given above), but in such fashion that any short notes that would go beyond the given scheme of harmonic density will occur only as non-chord tones. In this way the feeling of motion necessary to this sort of theme can be combined with the conciseness desirable for the principal material of a movement.

Section B, on the other hand, should be as free as possible of in-

[44]

dependent lines, both times it appears; only in measures 60-67 might the play of line become slightly more developed, in order to give emphasis to the repetition of the theme.

The climax, C, needs a good deal of part-motion, but not much independence in the lines. So here one should try as far as possible to let the quarter-notes called for in the plan of harmonic density fall on chord tones.

Section D, if it is to be realized as planned, can only be entirely homophonic.

For the two appearances of the transition, E, the style is already prescribed: the effect, in spite of the juxtaposition of the rhythms ♩ ♩ ♩̑♩ ♩ ♩ and ♩ ♪♩ ♪ , is not markedly contrapuntal. For since the texture of this passage has only limited melodic interest, the chief impression of which the listener is conscious is the jerky rhythmic impulsion.

Finally, Section F, in order to make the contrast between the climax and the restatement of the principal theme perfectly clear, should attain the relatively highest degree of contrapuntal energy in this piece—the continual changes of harmony in quarter-notes called for in the plan of harmonic density hardly permit of any other interpretation. In this section, three thoroughly independent melodic lines should move freely, and only draw together toward the end (measures 46-47) for a homophonic, cadential effect.

There is an additional factor of construction on which the style of the piece depends, for which I would like to use the term *Layers*. By this is meant the *vertical* strata of the harmonic texture as opposed to the *horizontal* plan of harmonic density: the word, layers, then, is to denote the number of tones, piled up above the lowest tone, of which the individual harmonies consist, and the rate of such increase or decrease in chordal mass as there may be in the progression from harmony to harmony. In pieces written in real parts, such as the present one, there is a choice between passages of thinnest texture for which occasionally two-part or even one-part writing may serve, and those of massive texture in which, with the aid of double stops, seven, eight, or more tones (counting doublings, of course) form a single harmony. The layers are thus determined by the number of independent single voices of which the coincident tones form chords, as well as by the number of mere chord tones which are part of the individual harmonies without belonging to actual horizontal voice lines. In this suite the layers will depend more on the first principle of construction just mentioned, whereas in compositions for piano—in which broken

chords constitute one of the outstanding features of the texture—
the second of the two principles is more likely to determine the style
(see the sonata movements later in the book).

The following plan may serve as a guide for working out the
layers. The number of lines indicates—approximately—the number of
real parts. Five lines indicate a very thick texture in which the chords
may contain even more than five tones.

Da capo al Fine

## Two Fugatos for Two Voices

1. **His Epitaph**        **Sir Walter Raleigh** (1552-1618)
   *for Soprano and Alto or Tenor and Bass*

2. **The Old Familiar Faces**        **Charles Lamb** (1775-1834)
   *for Tenor and Bass*

With these fugatos and the little fugues that follow them, an attempt is made to initiate the student in unorthodox fashion into the technique of fugue-writing. These few examples cannot of course clear away the whole miserable collection of unmusical formulas—the dreary and lifeless pasting together of "expositions" and "episodes"— of which the usual instruction in fugue consists. But they seek to demonstrate that instead of the usual approach to fugue—namely, by way of style-imitation, of Palestrina in vocal music, and of Bach in instrumental—a working method can be developed that concerns itself less with questions of style than with the essentially technical treatment of the material. There is no single, hard-and-fast style that must be followed in fugues any more than in other musical forms. If a student is advanced enough to write fugues, he must also be capable of working out a style that will suit his musical material, his conception of the complete piece, and the performance purposes he has in mind. Ideally, of course, he could only do this if he were to develop his own thematic and structural ideas from the first note on. But this requires considerable proficiency which can be acquired only by plentiful preparatory exercises. My conception of the nature of such preparatory exercises is shown in the following examples. Many more exercises of this sort are necessary to lay a solid technical foundation for the work of future contrapuntalists. The few examples given here are intended to stimulate the teacher to invent further material of the same sort for his students, seeing to it that, as the proficiency of the student increases, the proportion of preparatory work on the part of the teacher in writing the fugal skeletons steadily diminishes and the student's share constantly grows.

Our fugatos and fugues are to be worked out according to the model procedure laid down for the first movement of the preceding string suite. Since there everything was described in great detail, the following remarks are to be regarded not as precise working instructions but rather as stimuli to the student's own productive reflection.

[54]

Complete the two fugatos for the two indicated voices.

*Form.* The first fugato consists of three separate little fugues that are to be differentiated in character from one another. The voice that sings a counterpoint to the theme at any moment must not rise above a certain level of melodic content, so that the theme—itself of little significance in these examples—can still be felt to be of primary interest. As will easily be seen, the second fugato contains only two contrasted sections.

*Tonality.* The tonal plan of each piece is clear from the sketch. In the first fugato, be sparing in the use of secondary dominants and secondary leading-tone effects in the third section ("yet from this earth"), since they might easily disturb the smooth tonal flow of the piece.

*Tonal Amplitude.* Although one cannot do much harm with only two voices, it is wise to calculate the amplitude. In this respect, too, the third section of the first fugato offers some problems.

*Harmonic Fluctuation* hardly plays any role in two-part vocal writing, since for the sake of making the pieces really singable (try them out!) one cannot get too far from the basic intervals of octave, fifth, fourth, thirds, and sixths.

*Harmonic Density.* It will be best for the changes of harmony to take place in half-notes in the first fugato and in quarter-notes in the second.

When both fugatos have been written out for two voices, and sung, provide them with a piano accompaniment that will serve to support the voices without in any way dominating them.

# 1. His Epitaph
Soprano and Alto (or Tenor and Bass)

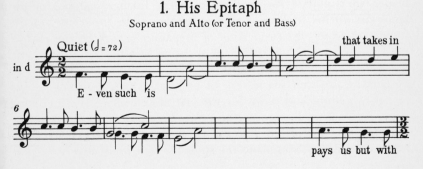

*Text:* Even such is Time, that takes in trust
Our youth, our joys, and all we have,
And pays us but with age and dust;
Who, in the dark and silent grave,
When we have wander'd all our ways,
Shuts up the story of our days;
But from this earth, this grave, this dust,
My God shall raise me up, I trust.

## 2. The Old Familiar Faces
Tenor and Bass

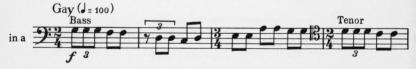

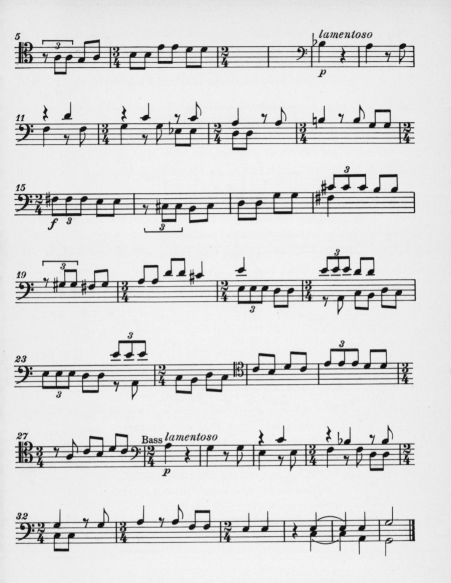

Text: I have had playmates, I have had companions,
In my days of childhood, in my joyful school-days—
All, all are gone, the old familiar faces.

I have been laughing, I have been carousing,
Drinking late, sitting late, with my bosom cronies—
All, all are gone, the old familiar faces.

## Two Two-Part Instrumental Fugues

### 1. Fugue for Piano
### 2. Fugue for Viola and 'Cello

Neither piece offers any problems of form. The theme of the second fugue, after several appearances in its original form, also occurs in inversion (measures 9, 13, 15, 21).

As regards tonality, one will have to guard against rapid modulations. The measures between two clearly recognizable tonal domains should therefore be kept as neutral as possible.

The harmonic density in the first fugue should not include any note-values shorter than the ♩. (even non-chord eighth-notes should be used very sparingly), and in the second the pulse will be given by progressions of harmony in eighth-notes.

1. Fast (♩.= 152)    For Piano

in A

For Viola and 'Cello

2. Scherzando (♪ = 112)

### Three Three-Part Vocal Fugues

**1. Melior est pauper**
*for Soprano, Alto, and Tenor*

**2. Omnis sapientia**
*for Soprano, Alto, and Bass*

**3. Justus germinabit**
*for Alto, Tenor, and Bass*

Here, too, be on guard against sudden or unbalanced modulations. Note-values of the harmonic density: first fugue ♩ ; second ♩. ; third ♩. .

### 1. Melior est pauper
Soprano, Alto, Tenor

Me-li- or       Me- li- or       Me- li- or

U - bi non est sci - en - ti - a

U - bi     U - bi

U - bi

et qui fe - sti - nus est___ pe - di-bus of - fen - - det.

**Text:** Melior est pauper, qui ambulat in simplicitate sua,
quam dives torquens labia sua, et insipiens.
Ubi non est scientia animæ, non est bonum:
et qui festinus est pedibus, offendet.

*Translation:*
Better is the poor that walketh in his integrity,
than he that is perverse in his lips, and is a fool.
Also, that the soul be without knowledge, it is not good;
and he that hasteth with his feet sinneth.
(*Proverbs*, xix, 1-2)

## 2. Omnis sapientia

Soprano, Alto, Bass

O- - mnis sa- pi- en- - ti - a a Do-mi-no De-
- -o O- - mnis

*Text:* Omnis sapientia a Domino Deo est,
et cum illo fuit semper, et est ante ævum.

*Translation:*

All wisdom is from the Lord God,
and hath been always with him, and is before all time.
(*Ecclesiasticus [Apocrypha], i,1*)

### 3. Justus germinabit
Alto, Tenor, Bass

*Text:* Justus germinabit sicut lilium:
et florebit in æternum ante Dominum.

*Translation:*

The just man shall blossom as the lily;
and he shall flourish in eternity before God.

(*Hosea,* xiv, 6)

## First Movement of a Sonata for Clarinet and Piano

For the following three pieces no specific instructions are given. Before beginning to work them out, the student must undertake all the preliminary investigations that have served as a basis for technical procedures in the preceding pieces.

Again, as in all the foregoing exercises, he must look with scorn on mere paper work. Nothing counts but the realization of the completed work *in sound*. It may not always be possible to enlist the services of a clarinet, a horn, or a string quartet, but with a little ingenuity it should not be difficult to find substitutes and perform the pieces.

The following clarinet sonata movement is conceived for a clarinet in B♭. The sketch, however, is written in C, so that in working out the piece the clarinet part will have to be rewritten in B♭.

# First Movement of a Sonata for Horn and Piano

The horn part is here notated in F.

# Theme and Variations for String Quartet

add a Coda of about 8 to 12 measures